The Closet Book
My Record Book of Prayers

PEACE

**by
KR Martin**

Copyright © 2021 by Martin & Clark, LLC

THE HOLY BIBLE, NEW INTERNATIONAL VERSION®, NIV® Copyright © 1973, 1978, 1984, 2011 by Biblica, Inc.™ Used by permission.

All rights reserved worldwide.

ISBN

    Wire-O Softcover: 978-1-957029-00-9

    Softcover / Paperback: 978-1-957029-01-6

DEDICATION

This book is dedicated to my birth sister, Teresa Martin Brown, who prayed me to every victory and through every trial. And to my spiritual sister, Yvonne Clark, whose constant efforts to memorize God's word have both challenged and inspired me.

January, 20_ _
During this month, do your best to memorize this verse.

Do not be anxious about anything, but in every situation, by prayer and petition, with thanksgiving, present your requests to God. And the peace of God, which transcends all understanding, will guard your hearts and your minds in Christ Jesus.
(Philippians 4: 6-7, NIV)

Write your featured month verse here. Dissect the verse and re-write it using your own words. Doodle the verse. Print it. Repeat it as often as possible.

✶ Personal ✶

My Thanksgiving... _____
_____
_____

My Repentance... _____
_____
_____

My Needs... _____
_____
_____

My Worries... _____
_____
_____

My Desires... _____
_____
_____

Who I need to forgive... _____
_____
_____

✴ My Family ✴

Family Name: _____

Concern: _____

Date Answered: _____

Family Name: _____

Concern: _____

Date Answered: _____

Family Name: _____

Concern: _____

Date Answered: _____

Family Name: _____

Concern: _____

Date Answered: _____

Family Name: _____

Concern: _____

Date Answered: _____

Family Name: _____

Concern: _____

Date Answered: _____

Family Name: _____

Concern: _____

Date Answered: _____

Family Name: _____

Concern: _____

Date Answered: _____

Family Name: _____

Concern: _____

Date Answered: _____

Family Name: _____

Concern: _____

Date Answered: _____

✻ My Friends ✻

Friend's Name: _____

Concern: _____

Date Answered: _____

Friend's Name: _____

Concern: _____

Date Answered: _____

Friend's Name: _____

Concern: _____

Date Answered: _____

Friend's Name: _____

Concern: _____

Date Answered: _____

Friend's Name: _____

Concern: _____

Date Answered: _____

Friend's Name: _____

Concern: _____

Date Answered: _____

Friend's Name: _____

Concern: _____

Date Answered: _____

Friend's Name: _____

Concern: _____

Date Answered: _____

Friend's Name: _____

Concern: _____

Date Answered: _____

Friend's Name: _____

Concern: _____

Date Answered: _____

✶ Prayers Requested by Others ✶

Name: _____

Concern: _____

Date Answered: _____

Name: _____

Concern: _____

Date Answered: _____

Name: _____

Concern: _____

Date Answered: _____

Name: _____

Concern: _____

Date Answered: _____

Name: _____

Concern: _____

Date Answered: _____

Name: _____

Concern: _____

Date Answered: _____

Name: _____

Concern: _____

Date Answered: _____

Name: _____

Concern: _____

Date Answered: _____

Name: _____

Concern: _____

Date Answered: _____

Name: _____

Concern: _____

Date Answered: _____

✶ *Scribble your thoughts...* ✶

February, 20____
During this month, do your best to memorize this verse.

For I am convinced that neither death nor life, neither angels nor demons, neither the present nor the future, nor any powers, neither height nor depth, nor anything else in all creation, will be able to separate us from the love of God that is in Christ Jesus our Lord.
(Romans 8:38-39, NIV)

Write your featured month verse here. Dissect the verse and re-write it using your own words. Doodle the verse. Print it. Repeat it as often as possible.

✶ Personal ✶

My Thanksgiving... _____
_____
_____

My Repentance... _____
_____
_____

My Needs... _____
_____
_____

My Worries... _____
_____
_____

My Desires... _____
_____
_____

Who I need to forgive... _____
_____
_____

✶ My Family ✶

Family Name: _____

Concern: _____

Date Answered: _____

Family Name: _____

Concern: _____

Date Answered: _____

Family Name: _____

Concern: _____

Date Answered: _____

Family Name: _____

Concern: _____

Date Answered: _____

Family Name: _____

Concern: _____

Date Answered: _____

Family Name: _____

Concern: _____

Date Answered: _____

Family Name: _____

Concern: _____

Date Answered: _____

Family Name: _____

Concern: _____

Date Answered: _____

Family Name: _____

Concern: _____

Date Answered: _____

Family Name: _____

Concern: _____

Date Answered: _____

✶ My Friends ✶

Friend's Name: _____

Concern: _____

Date Answered: _____

Friend's Name: _____

Concern: _____

Date Answered: _____

Friend's Name: _____

Concern: _____

Date Answered: _____

Friend's Name: _____

Concern: _____

Date Answered: _____

Friend's Name: _____

Concern: _____

Date Answered: _____

Friend's Name: _____

Concern: _____

Date Answered: _____

Friend's Name: _____

Concern: _____

Date Answered: _____

Friend's Name: _____

Concern: _____

Date Answered: _____

Friend's Name: _____

Concern: _____

Date Answered: _____

Friend's Name: _____

Concern: _____

Date Answered: _____

✶ Prayers Requested by Others ✶

Name: _____   Name: _____

Concern: _____   Concern: _____

Date Answered: _____   Date Answered: _____

Name: _____   Name: _____

Concern: _____   Concern: _____

Date Answered: _____   Date Answered: _____

Name: _____   Name: _____

Concern: _____   Concern: _____

Date Answered: _____   Date Answered: _____

Name: _____   Name: _____

Concern: _____   Concern: _____

Date Answered: _____   Date Answered: _____

Name: _____   Name: _____

Concern: _____   Concern: _____

Date Answered: _____   Date Answered: _____

Scribble your thoughts...

March, 20____
During this month, do your best to memorize this verse.

I keep my eyes always on the Lord.
With him at my right hand, I will not be shaken.
(Psalm 16:8, NIV)

Write your featured month verse here. Dissect the verse and re-write it using your own words. Doodle the verse. Print it. Repeat it as often as possible.

✶ Personal ✶

My Thanksgiving... _____
_____
_____

My Repentance... _____
_____
_____

My Needs... _____
_____
_____

My Worries... _____
_____
_____

My Desires... _____
_____
_____

Who I need to forgive... _____
_____
_____

✳ My Family ✳

Family Name: _____

Concern: _____

Date Answered: _____

Family Name: _____

Concern: _____

Date Answered: _____

Family Name: _____

Concern: _____

Date Answered: _____

Family Name: _____

Concern: _____

Date Answered: _____

Family Name: _____

Concern: _____

Date Answered: _____

Family Name: _____

Concern: _____

Date Answered: _____

Family Name: _____

Concern: _____

Date Answered: _____

Family Name: _____

Concern: _____

Date Answered: _____

Family Name: _____

Concern: _____

Date Answered: _____

Family Name: _____

Concern: _____

Date Answered: _____

✶ My Friends ✶

Friend's Name: _____ Friend's Name: _____

Concern: _____ Concern: _____

Date Answered: _____ Date Answered: _____

Friend's Name: _____ Friend's Name: _____

Concern: _____ Concern: _____

Date Answered: _____ Date Answered: _____

Friend's Name: _____ Friend's Name: _____

Concern: _____ Concern: _____

Date Answered: _____ Date Answered: _____

Friend's Name: _____ Friend's Name: _____

Concern: _____ Concern: _____

Date Answered: _____ Date Answered: _____

Friend's Name: _____ Friend's Name: _____

Concern: _____ Concern: _____

Date Answered: _____ Date Answered: _____

✳ Prayers Requested by Others ✳

Name: _____

Concern: _____

Date Answered: _____

Name: _____

Concern: _____

Date Answered: _____

Name: _____

Concern: _____

Date Answered: _____

Name: _____

Concern: _____

Date Answered: _____

Name: _____

Concern: _____

Date Answered: _____

Name: _____

Concern: _____

Date Answered: _____

Name: _____

Concern: _____

Date Answered: _____

Name: _____

Concern: _____

Date Answered: _____

Name: _____

Concern: _____

Date Answered: _____

Name: _____

Concern: _____

Date Answered: _____

✦ *Scribble your thoughts...* ✦

Lord,
I sometimes take my eyes off You and focus on worries, pressures, fears, and frustrations. I often set my eyes on myself, others, or on the wonderful things I have, want or love to do. Help me to keep You as my focus then nothing can shake me.

April, 20____
During this month, do your best to memorize this verse.

*Whoever dwells in the shelter of the Most High
will rest in the shadow of the Almighty.
I will say of the Lord,
"He is my refuge and my fortress,
my God, in whom I trust."
(Psalm 91:1-2, NIV)*

Write your featured month verse here. Dissect the verse and re-write it using your own words. Doodle the verse. Print it. Repeat it as often as possible.

✶ Personal ✶

My Thanksgiving... _____
_____
_____

My Repentance... _____
_____
_____

My Needs... _____
_____
_____

My Worries... _____
_____
_____

My Desires... _____
_____
_____

Who I need to forgive... _____
_____
_____

✶ My Family ✶

Family Name: _____

Concern: _____

Date Answered: _____

Family Name: _____

Concern: _____

Date Answered: _____

Family Name: _____

Concern: _____

Date Answered: _____

Family Name: _____

Concern: _____

Date Answered: _____

Family Name: _____

Concern: _____

Date Answered: _____

Family Name: _____

Concern: _____

Date Answered: _____

Family Name: _____

Concern: _____

Date Answered: _____

Family Name: _____

Concern: _____

Date Answered: _____

Family Name: _____

Concern: _____

Date Answered: _____

Family Name: _____

Concern: _____

Date Answered: _____

✶ My Friends ✶

Friend's Name: _____

Concern: _____

Date Answered: _____

Friend's Name: _____

Concern: _____

Date Answered: _____

Friend's Name: _____

Concern: _____

Date Answered: _____

Friend's Name: _____

Concern: _____

Date Answered: _____

Friend's Name: _____

Concern: _____

Date Answered: _____

Friend's Name: _____

Concern: _____

Date Answered: _____

Friend's Name: _____

Concern: _____

Date Answered: _____

Friend's Name: _____

Concern: _____

Date Answered: _____

Friend's Name: _____

Concern: _____

Date Answered: _____

Friend's Name: _____

Concern: _____

Date Answered: _____

✳ Prayers Requested by Others ✳

Name: _____

Concern: _____

Date Answered: _____

Name: _____

Concern: _____

Date Answered: _____

Name: _____

Concern: _____

Date Answered: _____

Name: _____

Concern: _____

Date Answered: _____

Name: _____

Concern: _____

Date Answered: _____

Name: _____

Concern: _____

Date Answered: _____

Name: _____

Concern: _____

Date Answered: _____

Name: _____

Concern: _____

Date Answered: _____

Name: _____

Concern: _____

Date Answered: _____

Name: _____

Concern: _____

Date Answered: _____

✷ *Scribble your thoughts...* ✷

LORD,

Help me to find security in You. I will turn to You when I feel vulnerable and under attack. When my spirit is tired, help me to find rest by drawing closer to You. I proclaim that You are my refuge and my protector. Above all, I will trust in You, my **GOD**.

May, 20____
During this month, do your best to memorize this verse.

Then Jesus said to his disciples: "Therefore I tell you, do not worry about your life, what you will eat; or about your body, what you will wear. For life is more than food, and the body more than clothes. Consider the ravens: They do not sow or reap, they have no storeroom or barn; yet God feeds them. And how much more valuable you are than birds! Who of you by worrying can add a single hour to your life? Since you cannot do this very little thing, why do you worry about the rest?
(Luke 12:22-26, NIV)

Write your featured month verse here. Dissect the verse and re-write it using your own words. Doodle the verse. Print it. Repeat it as often as possible.

_____
_____
_____
_____
_____
_____
_____
_____
_____
_____
_____
_____
_____
_____
_____
_____
_____

✶ Personal ✶

My Thanksgiving... _____
_____
_____

My Repentance... _____
_____
_____

My Needs... _____
_____
_____

My Worries... _____
_____
_____

My Desires... _____
_____
_____

Who I need to forgive... _____
_____
_____

✶ My Family ✶

Family Name: _____   Family Name: _____

Concern: _____   Concern: _____

Date Answered: _____   Date Answered: _____

Family Name: _____   Family Name: _____

Concern: _____   Concern: _____

Date Answered: _____   Date Answered: _____

Family Name: _____   Family Name: _____

Concern: _____   Concern: _____

Date Answered: _____   Date Answered: _____

Family Name: _____   Family Name: _____

Concern: _____   Concern: _____

Date Answered: _____   Date Answered: _____

Family Name: _____   Family Name: _____

Concern: _____   Concern: _____

Date Answered: _____   Date Answered: _____

✷ My Friends ✷

Friend's Name: _____

Concern: _____

Date Answered: _____

Friend's Name: _____

Concern: _____

Date Answered: _____

Friend's Name: _____

Concern: _____

Date Answered: _____

Friend's Name: _____

Concern: _____

Date Answered: _____

Friend's Name: _____

Concern: _____

Date Answered: _____

Friend's Name: _____

Concern: _____

Date Answered: _____

Friend's Name: _____

Concern: _____

Date Answered: _____

Friend's Name: _____

Concern: _____

Date Answered: _____

Friend's Name: _____

Concern: _____

Date Answered: _____

Friend's Name: _____

Concern: _____

Date Answered: _____

✶ Prayers Requested by Others ✶

Name: _____

Concern: _____

Date Answered: _____

Name: _____

Concern: _____

Date Answered: _____

Name: _____

Concern: _____

Date Answered: _____

Name: _____

Concern: _____

Date Answered: _____

Name: _____

Concern: _____

Date Answered: _____

Name: _____

Concern: _____

Date Answered: _____

Name: _____

Concern: _____

Date Answered: _____

Name: _____

Concern: _____

Date Answered: _____

Name: _____

Concern: _____

Date Answered: _____

Name: _____

Concern: _____

Date Answered: _____

✲ *Scribble your thoughts...* ✲

Lord,

Worry has never fixed anything. It creates misery. When I start to worry, help me to calm my mind and put aside things I have imagined but might never happen. Help me to discern the real issues, take wise actions and then simply trust

you.

June, 20____
During this month, do your best to memorize this verse.

*Anxiety weighs down the heart,
but a kind word cheers it up.
(Proverbs 12:25, NIV)*

Write your featured month verse here. Dissect the verse and re-write it using your own words. Doodle the verse. Print it. Repeat it as often as possible.

_____
_____
_____
_____
_____
_____
_____
_____
_____
_____
_____
_____
_____
_____
_____
_____
_____

✶ Personal ✶

My Thanksgiving... _____
_____
_____

My Repentance... _____
_____
_____

My Needs... _____
_____
_____

My Worries... _____
_____
_____

My Desires... _____
_____
_____

Who I need to forgive... _____
_____
_____

✷ My Family ✷

Family Name: _____

Concern: _____

Date Answered: _____

Family Name: _____

Concern: _____

Date Answered: _____

Family Name: _____

Concern: _____

Date Answered: _____

Family Name: _____

Concern: _____

Date Answered: _____

Family Name: _____

Concern: _____

Date Answered: _____

Family Name: _____

Concern: _____

Date Answered: _____

Family Name: _____

Concern: _____

Date Answered: _____

Family Name: _____

Concern: _____

Date Answered: _____

Family Name: _____

Concern: _____

Date Answered: _____

Family Name: _____

Concern: _____

Date Answered: _____

✶ My Friends ✶

Friend's Name: _____

Concern: _____

Date Answered: _____

Friend's Name: _____

Concern: _____

Date Answered: _____

Friend's Name: _____

Concern: _____

Date Answered: _____

Friend's Name: _____

Concern: _____

Date Answered: _____

Friend's Name: _____

Concern: _____

Date Answered: _____

Friend's Name: _____

Concern: _____

Date Answered: _____

Friend's Name: _____

Concern: _____

Date Answered: _____

Friend's Name: _____

Concern: _____

Date Answered: _____

Friend's Name: _____

Concern: _____

Date Answered: _____

Friend's Name: _____

Concern: _____

Date Answered: _____

✳ Prayers Requested by Others ✳

Name: _____

Concern: _____

Date Answered: _____

Name: _____

Concern: _____

Date Answered: _____

Name: _____

Concern: _____

Date Answered: _____

Name: _____

Concern: _____

Date Answered: _____

Name: _____

Concern: _____

Date Answered: _____

Name: _____

Concern: _____

Date Answered: _____

Name: _____

Concern: _____

Date Answered: _____

Name: _____

Concern: _____

Date Answered: _____

Name: _____

Concern: _____

Date Answered: _____

Name: _____

Concern: _____

Date Answered: _____

✶ *Scribble your thoughts...* ✶

July, 20__ __
During this month, do your best to memorize this verse.

I have told you these things,
so that in me you may have peace.
In this world you will have trouble.
But take heart!
I have overcome the world.
(John 16:33, NIV)

Write your featured month verse here. Dissect the verse and re-write it using your own words. Doodle the verse. Print it. Repeat it as often as possible.

✶ Personal ✶

My Thanksgiving... _____
_____
_____

My Repentance... _____
_____
_____

My Needs... _____
_____
_____

My Worries... _____
_____
_____

My Desires... _____
_____
_____

Who I need to forgive... _____
_____
_____

✶ My Family ✶

Family Name: _____   Family Name: _____

Concern: _____   Concern: _____

Date Answered: _____   Date Answered: _____

Family Name: _____   Family Name: _____

Concern: _____   Concern: _____

Date Answered: _____   Date Answered: _____

Family Name: _____   Family Name: _____

Concern: _____   Concern: _____

Date Answered: _____   Date Answered: _____

Family Name: _____   Family Name: _____

Concern: _____   Concern: _____

Date Answered: _____   Date Answered: _____

Family Name: _____   Family Name: _____

Concern: _____   Concern: _____

Date Answered: _____   Date Answered: _____

✶ My Friends ✶

Friend's Name: _____

Concern: _____

Date Answered: _____

Friend's Name: _____

Concern: _____

Date Answered: _____

Friend's Name: _____

Concern: _____

Date Answered: _____

Friend's Name: _____

Concern: _____

Date Answered: _____

Friend's Name: _____

Concern: _____

Date Answered: _____

Friend's Name: _____

Concern: _____

Date Answered: _____

Friend's Name: _____

Concern: _____

Date Answered: _____

Friend's Name: _____

Concern: _____

Date Answered: _____

Friend's Name: _____

Concern: _____

Date Answered: _____

Friend's Name: _____

Concern: _____

Date Answered: _____

✷ Prayers Requested by Others ✷

Name: _____

Concern: _____

Date Answered: _____

Name: _____

Concern: _____

Date Answered: _____

Name: _____

Concern: _____

Date Answered: _____

Name: _____

Concern: _____

Date Answered: _____

Name: _____

Concern: _____

Date Answered: _____

Name: _____

Concern: _____

Date Answered: _____

Name: _____

Concern: _____

Date Answered: _____

Name: _____

Concern: _____

Date Answered: _____

Name: _____

Concern: _____

Date Answered: _____

Name: _____

Concern: _____

Date Answered: _____

✴ *Scribble your thoughts...* ✴

Lord,

You want me to have peace in my life. That is clear in Your Word. I can anticipate troubles in this world, but they won't last forever. Your Word and promises will last forever. Help me to live in victory because You have overcome the world and I am Yours.

August, 20____
During this month, do your best to memorize this verse.

Humble yourselves, therefore, under God's mighty hand, that he may lift you up in due time. Cast all your anxiety on him because he cares for you.
(1 Peter 5:6-7, NIV)

Write your featured month verse here. Dissect the verse and re-write it using your own words. Doodle the verse. Print it. Repeat it as often as possible.

✶ Personal ✶

My Thanksgiving... _____
_____
_____

My Repentance... _____
_____
_____

My Needs... _____
_____
_____

My Worries... _____
_____
_____

My Desires... _____
_____
_____

Who I need to forgive... _____
_____
_____

✻ My Family ✻

Family Name: _____

Concern: _____

Date Answered: _____

Family Name: _____

Concern: _____

Date Answered: _____

Family Name: _____

Concern: _____

Date Answered: _____

Family Name: _____

Concern: _____

Date Answered: _____

Family Name: _____

Concern: _____

Date Answered: _____

Family Name: _____

Concern: _____

Date Answered: _____

Family Name: _____

Concern: _____

Date Answered: _____

Family Name: _____

Concern: _____

Date Answered: _____

Family Name: _____

Concern: _____

Date Answered: _____

Family Name: _____

Concern: _____

Date Answered: _____

✶ My Friends ✶

Friend's Name: _____

Concern: _____

Date Answered: _____

Friend's Name: _____

Concern: _____

Date Answered: _____

Friend's Name: _____

Concern: _____

Date Answered: _____

Friend's Name: _____

Concern: _____

Date Answered: _____

Friend's Name: _____

Concern: _____

Date Answered: _____

Friend's Name: _____

Concern: _____

Date Answered: _____

Friend's Name: _____

Concern: _____

Date Answered: _____

Friend's Name: _____

Concern: _____

Date Answered: _____

Friend's Name: _____

Concern: _____

Date Answered: _____

Friend's Name: _____

Concern: _____

Date Answered: _____

✸ Prayers Requested by Others ✸

Name: _____

Concern: _____

Date Answered: _____

Name: _____

Concern: _____

Date Answered: _____

Name: _____

Concern: _____

Date Answered: _____

Name: _____

Concern: _____

Date Answered: _____

Name: _____

Concern: _____

Date Answered: _____

Name: _____

Concern: _____

Date Answered: _____

Name: _____

Concern: _____

Date Answered: _____

Name: _____

Concern: _____

Date Answered: _____

Name: _____

Concern: _____

Date Answered: _____

Name: _____

Concern: _____

Date Answered: _____

✴ *Scribble your thoughts...* ✴

LORD,

Sometimes I feel that I bear the burden of all the problems around me. They weigh me down. Help me to come to You in humility and admit that I can't fix everything. I bring my worries to You because You care for me. Your timing is perfect.

September, 20____

During this month, do your best to memorize this verse.

*When I said, "My foot is slipping,"
your unfailing love, Lord, supported me.
When anxiety was great within me,
your consolation brought me joy.
(Psalm 94:18-19, NIV)*

Write your featured month verse here. Dissect the verse and re-write it using your own words. Doodle the verse. Print it. Repeat it as often as possible.

✶ Personal ✶

My Thanksgiving... _____
_____
_____

My Repentance... _____
_____
_____

My Needs... _____
_____
_____

My Worries... _____
_____
_____

My Desires... _____
_____
_____

Who I need to forgive... _____
_____
_____

✶ My Family ✶

Family Name: _____

Concern: _____

Date Answered: _____

Family Name: _____

Concern: _____

Date Answered: _____

Family Name: _____

Concern: _____

Date Answered: _____

Family Name: _____

Concern: _____

Date Answered: _____

Family Name: _____

Concern: _____

Date Answered: _____

Family Name: _____

Concern: _____

Date Answered: _____

Family Name: _____

Concern: _____

Date Answered: _____

Family Name: _____

Concern: _____

Date Answered: _____

Family Name: _____

Concern: _____

Date Answered: _____

Family Name: _____

Concern: _____

Date Answered: _____

✶ My Friends ✶

Friend's Name: _____

Concern: _____

Date Answered: _____

Friend's Name: _____

Concern: _____

Date Answered: _____

Friend's Name: _____

Concern: _____

Date Answered: _____

Friend's Name: _____

Concern: _____

Date Answered: _____

Friend's Name: _____

Concern: _____

Date Answered: _____

Friend's Name: _____

Concern: _____

Date Answered: _____

Friend's Name: _____

Concern: _____

Date Answered: _____

Friend's Name: _____

Concern: _____

Date Answered: _____

Friend's Name: _____

Concern: _____

Date Answered: _____

Friend's Name: _____

Concern: _____

Date Answered: _____

✷ Prayers Requested by Others ✷

Name: _____

Concern: _____

Date Answered: _____

Name: _____

Concern: _____

Date Answered: _____

Name: _____

Concern: _____

Date Answered: _____

Name: _____

Concern: _____

Date Answered: _____

Name: _____

Concern: _____

Date Answered: _____

Name: _____

Concern: _____

Date Answered: _____

Name: _____

Concern: _____

Date Answered: _____

Name: _____

Concern: _____

Date Answered: _____

Name: _____

Concern: _____

Date Answered: _____

Name: _____

Concern: _____

Date Answered: _____

Scribble your thoughts...

Lord,

Help me to remember the times in my life when I felt I couldn't stand but You kept me from falling. When I am anxious, help me to recall the situations through which You have already delivered me. Your love never fails me. That brings me comfort and joy.

October, 20____

During this month, do your best to memorize this verse.

*Peace I leave with you; my peace I give you.
I do not give to you as the world gives.
Do not let your hearts be troubled
and do not be afraid.
(John 14:27, NIV)*

Write your featured month verse here. Dissect the verse and re-write it using your own words. Doodle the verse. Print it. Repeat it as often as possible.

✶ Personal ✶

My Thanksgiving... _____
_____
_____

My Repentance... _____
_____
_____

My Needs... _____
_____
_____

My Worries... _____
_____
_____

My Desires... _____
_____
_____

Who I need to forgive... _____
_____
_____

✶ My Family ✶

Family Name: _____

Concern: _____

Date Answered: _____

Family Name: _____

Concern: _____

Date Answered: _____

Family Name: _____

Concern: _____

Date Answered: _____

Family Name: _____

Concern: _____

Date Answered: _____

Family Name: _____

Concern: _____

Date Answered: _____

Family Name: _____

Concern: _____

Date Answered: _____

Family Name: _____

Concern: _____

Date Answered: _____

Family Name: _____

Concern: _____

Date Answered: _____

Family Name: _____

Concern: _____

Date Answered: _____

Family Name: _____

Concern: _____

Date Answered: _____

✶ My Friends ✶

Friend's Name: _____

Concern: _____

Date Answered: _____

Friend's Name: _____

Concern: _____

Date Answered: _____

Friend's Name: _____

Concern: _____

Date Answered: _____

Friend's Name: _____

Concern: _____

Date Answered: _____

Friend's Name: _____

Concern: _____

Date Answered: _____

Friend's Name: _____

Concern: _____

Date Answered: _____

Friend's Name: _____

Concern: _____

Date Answered: _____

Friend's Name: _____

Concern: _____

Date Answered: _____

Friend's Name: _____

Concern: _____

Date Answered: _____

Friend's Name: _____

Concern: _____

Date Answered: _____

✶ Prayers Requested by Others ✶

Name: _____

Concern: _____

Date Answered: _____

Name: _____

Concern: _____

Date Answered: _____

Name: _____

Concern: _____

Date Answered: _____

Name: _____

Concern: _____

Date Answered: _____

Name: _____

Concern: _____

Date Answered: _____

Name: _____

Concern: _____

Date Answered: _____

Name: _____

Concern: _____

Date Answered: _____

Name: _____

Concern: _____

Date Answered: _____

Name: _____

Concern: _____

Date Answered: _____

Name: _____

Concern: _____

Date Answered: _____

✶ *Scribble your thoughts...* ✶

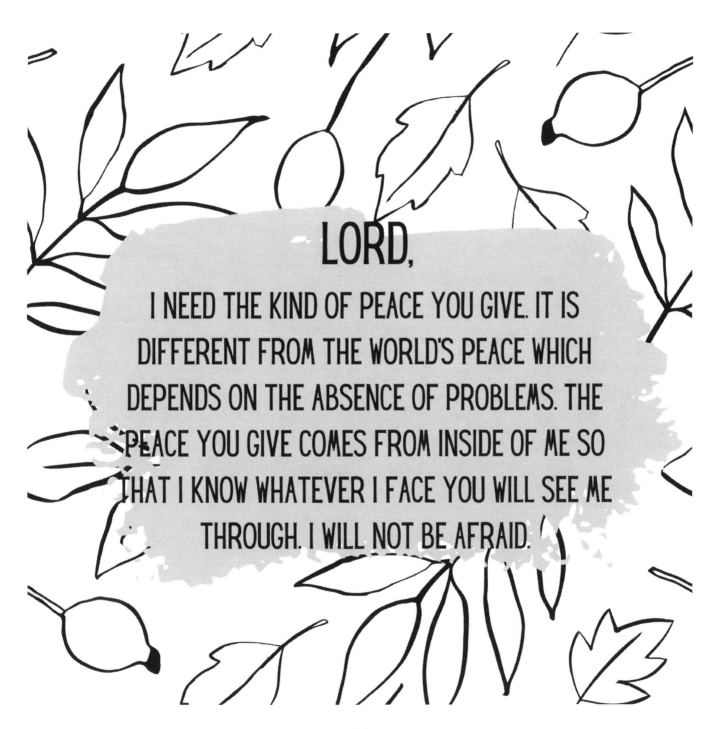

LORD,

I NEED THE KIND OF PEACE YOU GIVE. IT IS DIFFERENT FROM THE WORLD'S PEACE WHICH DEPENDS ON THE ABSENCE OF PROBLEMS. THE PEACE YOU GIVE COMES FROM INSIDE OF ME SO THAT I KNOW WHATEVER I FACE YOU WILL SEE ME THROUGH. I WILL NOT BE AFRAID.

November, 20____
During this month, do your best to memorize this verse.

*And we know that in all things
God works for the good of those who love him,
who have been called according to his purpose.
(Romans 8:28, NIV)*

Write your featured month verse here. Dissect the verse and re-write it using your own words. Doodle the verse. Print it. Repeat it as often as possible.

_____
_____
_____
_____
_____
_____
_____
_____
_____
_____
_____
_____
_____
_____
_____
_____
_____

✶ Personal ✶

My Thanksgiving... _____
_____
_____

My Repentance... _____
_____
_____

My Needs... _____
_____
_____

My Worries... _____
_____
_____

My Desires... _____
_____
_____

Who I need to forgive... _____
_____
_____

✶ My Family ✶

Family Name: _____

Concern: _____

Date Answered: _____

Family Name: _____

Concern: _____

Date Answered: _____

Family Name: _____

Concern: _____

Date Answered: _____

Family Name: _____

Concern: _____

Date Answered: _____

Family Name: _____

Concern: _____

Date Answered: _____

Family Name: _____

Concern: _____

Date Answered: _____

Family Name: _____

Concern: _____

Date Answered: _____

Family Name: _____

Concern: _____

Date Answered: _____

Family Name: _____

Concern: _____

Date Answered: _____

Family Name: _____

Concern: _____

Date Answered: _____

✶ My Friends ✶

Friend's Name: _____

Concern: _____

Date Answered: _____

Friend's Name: _____

Concern: _____

Date Answered: _____

Friend's Name: _____

Concern: _____

Date Answered: _____

Friend's Name: _____

Concern: _____

Date Answered: _____

Friend's Name: _____

Concern: _____

Date Answered: _____

Friend's Name: _____

Concern: _____

Date Answered: _____

Friend's Name: _____

Concern: _____

Date Answered: _____

Friend's Name: _____

Concern: _____

Date Answered: _____

Friend's Name: _____

Concern: _____

Date Answered: _____

Friend's Name: _____

Concern: _____

Date Answered: _____

✶ Prayers Requested by Others ✶

Name: _____

Concern: _____

Date Answered: _____

Name: _____

Concern: _____

Date Answered: _____

Name: _____

Concern: _____

Date Answered: _____

Name: _____

Concern: _____

Date Answered: _____

Name: _____

Concern: _____

Date Answered: _____

Name: _____

Concern: _____

Date Answered: _____

Name: _____

Concern: _____

Date Answered: _____

Name: _____

Concern: _____

Date Answered: _____

Name: _____

Concern: _____

Date Answered: _____

Name: _____

Concern: _____

Date Answered: _____

Scribble your thoughts...

Lord,
Regardless of what is going on, who did what to me, or how things turned out You have promised that You will bring good out of every circumstance

for us who genuinely love You. I am Your child, and You will help me to become all You mean for me to be.

December, 20__ __
During this month, do your best to memorize this verse.

*May God Himself, the God of peace,
sanctify you through and through.
May your whole spirit, soul and body be kept
blameless at the coming of our Lord Jesus Christ.
The one who calls you is faithful, and He will do it.
(1 Thessalonians 5: 23-24, NIV)*

Write your featured month verse here. Dissect the verse and re-write it using your own words. Doodle the verse. Print it. Repeat it as often as possible.

✷ Personal ✷

My Thanksgiving... _____
_____
_____

My Repentance... _____
_____
_____

My Needs... _____
_____
_____

My Worries... _____
_____
_____

My Desires... _____
_____
_____

Who I need to forgive... _____
_____
_____

✶ My Family ✶

Family Name: _____   Family Name: _____

Concern: _____   Concern: _____

Date Answered: _____   Date Answered: _____

Family Name: _____   Family Name: _____

Concern: _____   Concern: _____

Date Answered: _____   Date Answered: _____

Family Name: _____   Family Name: _____

Concern: _____   Concern: _____

Date Answered: _____   Date Answered: _____

Family Name: _____   Family Name: _____

Concern: _____   Concern: _____

Date Answered: _____   Date Answered: _____

Family Name: _____   Family Name: _____

Concern: _____   Concern: _____

Date Answered: _____   Date Answered: _____

✶ My Friends ✶

Friend's Name: _____

Concern: _____

Date Answered: _____

Friend's Name: _____

Concern: _____

Date Answered: _____

Friend's Name: _____

Concern: _____

Date Answered: _____

Friend's Name: _____

Concern: _____

Date Answered: _____

Friend's Name: _____

Concern: _____

Date Answered: _____

Friend's Name: _____

Concern: _____

Date Answered: _____

Friend's Name: _____

Concern: _____

Date Answered: _____

Friend's Name: _____

Concern: _____

Date Answered: _____

Friend's Name: _____

Concern: _____

Date Answered: _____

Friend's Name: _____

Concern: _____

Date Answered: _____

✶ Prayers Requested by Others ✶

Name: _____ Name: _____

Concern: _____ Concern: _____

Date Answered: _____ Date Answered: _____

Name: _____ Name: _____

Concern: _____ Concern: _____

Date Answered: _____ Date Answered: _____

Name: _____ Name: _____

Concern: _____ Concern: _____

Date Answered: _____ Date Answered: _____

Name: _____ Name: _____

Concern: _____ Concern: _____

Date Answered: _____ Date Answered: _____

Name: _____ Name: _____

Concern: _____ Concern: _____

Date Answered: _____ Date Answered: _____

✶ *Scribble your thoughts...* ✶

Lord,

Make me holy. Make me a living sanctuary where You abide. Convict me of pride and sin. Reveal my faults to me. Cause me to desire to be blameless so I can stand before You without shame. You can accomplish this in my life because You are faithful.

✶ *Important Thoughts and Notes* ✶

To experience an original Broadway-style production by Martin & Clark visit the NarroWay Theatre just outside of Charlotte NC at 3327 Hwy. 51, Fort Mill SC. Find NarroWay online at narroway.net or request information by phone at 803.802.2300.

Additional works by Martin & Clark available at narroway.net and martinandclark.com.

Made in the USA
Columbia, SC
27 November 2023